Written by

EMILIE
DUFRESNE

Designed by

BookLife
PUBLISHING

©This edition published 2021.
First published in 2020.

BookLife Publishing
King's Lynn
Norfolk PE30 4LS

All rights reserved.
Printed in Malta.

A catalogue record for this book is available from the British Library.

ISBN: 978-1-83927-082-6

Written by:
Emilie Dufresne

Edited by:
Madeline Tyler

Designed by:
Danielle Rippengill

Image Credits

All images are courtesy of Shutterstock.com, unless otherwise specified. With thanks to Getty Images, Thinkstock Photo and iStockphoto. Cover – cosmaa, View6424, Sundry Studio, Dvorko Sergey, Vextok. Heading typface used throughout – cosmaa. Images used on every page – cosmaa, Sundry Studio. 3 – Dvorko Sergey, Vextok. 8 – AndrewHeffernan. 11 – Sashatigar. 12 – Dvorko Sergey, Vextok. 13 – GoodStudio. 14 – VitalasArts. 15 – Grinbox. 22&23 – Mix3r. 27 – Skoreya.

CONTENTS

Words that look like this are explained in the glossary on page 30.

NASA

HAVING PRIDE

What Does It Mean to Have Pride?

Having pride or being proud is when you feel good or worthy because of who you are or the things you have done. You might feel proud of yourself or of other people and the things they have done.

What Is Pride?

As well as being a word to describe how people feel, Pride is also a <u>march</u> and celebration of people from the LGBTQIA+ <u>community</u>. Many towns and cities across the world hold Pride marches and celebrations. They are a time for people to celebrate who they are and remind people of what still needs to be achieved for people in the LGBTQIA+ community.

Pride In STEM

Some charities and organisations celebrate the LGBTQIA+ community working in certain areas. Pride in STEM is a charity that celebrates LGBTQIA+ people who work in STEM and tries to make positive changes for those people. STEM stands for science, technology, engineering and maths.

What Does LGBTQIA+ Mean?

The letters that make up LGBTQIA+ mean many different things about sex, sexuality and gender identity.

Sex

A person's sex is to do with their biology. It can refer to the biological sex they were assigned at birth, or it could be the sex they identify with.

Sexuality

Sexuality is a way of talking about a person's sexual identity. This is to do with the ways in which a person may or may not feel attracted to people, and what people they are attracted to.

Gender Identity

Gender identity is a person's idea of how they are masculine, feminine, a mixture of both of these, or neither of them.

A Closer Look at the Letters

Different people use different combinations of letters to talk about the LGBTQIA+ community. As we learn more about sex, sexuality and gender identity, more letters can be added to make sure everyone feels included in the community.

Bisexual
This is a person who is attracted to more than one gender.

Transgender
This is when a person's gender identity is different to the biological sex they were assigned at birth.

Gay
This can be men or women who are only attracted to people who are the same sex as them.

Lesbian
This is a woman who is only attracted to other women.

The LGBTQIA+ community is often represented by a rainbow flag. The flag celebrates the fact that even though we are all different, it is these differences that we should celebrate. It is time to share the pride of LGBTQIA+ people working in STEM.

Queer
Someone might see themselves as queer if they feel their sexual and gender identities are anything other than heterosexual or cisgender.

Intersex
This is a person who is born with a mixture of sex characteristics that are seen as male and female, such as genitals and chromosomes.

Asexual
This is a person who does not feel sexually attracted to any sex or gender.

Plus
This is used to include all the letters that are missing from the abbreviation and to make sure everyone in the LGBTQIA+ community feels included regardless of who they are. This can include people who are pansexual or gender fluid.

ALAN TURING

Cracking the Code

Alan Turing had a great mind from a young age, and during his school life he was constantly wanting to learn more. He went to the University of Cambridge to study maths. During World War Two, Turing was one of the people who helped to crack the codes to figure out enemy messages. In his later work, he went on to design one of the first electronic computers.

Those who can imagine anything, can create the impossible.

Finding His Fame

During Alan's lifetime, it was against the law to be gay in the UK. He was arrested and found guilty when it came out that he was having a relationship with a man. After his death, Alan was <u>pardoned</u> along with many other gay men who were convicted at that time. It was also only after his death that Alan's amazing work in computing and code breaking was celebrated.

Achievements

- Awarded an **OBE** for his services during World War Two
- Invented the Turing test, which tests whether **AI** is as intelligent as a human
- Invented one of the first electronic computers

Fighting the Law

Since 1967, the laws in the UK have changed and same-sex relationships are now legal. However, in many countries this is not the case. Many organisations and charities work to protect the **rights** of LGBTQIA+ people around the world. Unfortunately, lots still needs to be done to make sure the LGBTQIA+ community are protected by the law everywhere.

LYNN CONWAY

Born: 1938

> Parents who have transgender children are discovering that if they ... let that person blossom into who they need to be ... they often see a remarkable <u>flourishing</u> of lifeforce.

Master of the Microchip

Lynn Conway is a computer scientist and engineer. She is well known for creating a design for <u>computer chips</u>. This design made it easier to make computer chips much smaller. Without Lynn's work, the world would not have the computer technology, such as smartphones and laptops, that we have today.

Transitioning and Becoming a Transgender Activist

Lynn was assigned male at birth, but when growing up she often felt as though her gender did not match her biological sex. Lynn decided to transition in 1966. She did not tell the public about her transition and chose to only tell close family. For a long time, many people she worked with did not know that she was a transgender woman. Many years after her transition, Lynn decided to tell the public and become a transgender <u>activist</u>. She now works to protect the rights of transgender people working in STEM.

What Is Transitioning?

A transgender person may or may not choose to transition. Transitioning means a different thing to every person. It might involve medical transitioning, such as taking medication or having surgery. For someone else, it could involve telling friends and family, dressing differently and changing their name to one they feel suits them more.

Achievements

- Won a National Achievement Award from the Society of Women Engineers in 1990
- Became a member of the Electronic Design Hall of Fame in 2002
- Named one of Stonewall's 40 Transgender Heroes in 2009

SALLY RIDE

Born: 1951 Died: 2012

> Young girls need to see role models in whatever careers they may choose, just so they can picture themselves doing those jobs someday. You can't do what you can't see.

A Giant Leap for Womankind

Sally Ride had always been interested in science and studied physics at university for many years. She was very interested in astrophysics and she managed to become an astronaut for NASA. She did many different jobs as an astronaut, and one of these was operating the robotic arm on the space shuttle.

A Lasting Legacy

In her later years, Sally spent her life trying to get more young people, especially girls, into science and maths. She became a role model for many women who wanted to get into astrophysics. After Sally's death, her partner Tam O'Shaughnessy wrote her obituary telling the public that Sally was gay. She did not choose to come out sooner than this because of the obstacles that some groups of people, including the LGBTQIA+ community, faced while working in STEM at this time.

Achievements

- First American woman in space

- Awarded the Presidential Medal of Freedom in 2013 after her death

- Co-founded Sally Ride Science, a science company that aims to inspire young people in STEM

What Is Coming Out?

Coming out is when a person chooses to tell someone about their sex, sexuality or gender identity. It is important to remember that a person doesn't have to come out unless they want to or are ready to. A person also doesn't have to come out to everyone they know at once — they can come out to whoever they want, whenever they want. The choice is theirs.

ROBOTIC ARM

UNITED STATES

NASA

BEN BARRES

Born: 1954 Died: 2017

Barres on the Brain

Ben Barres was a <u>neurobiologist</u> who spent a lot of his career studying a type of <u>cell</u> called glia, which are found in the brain. For a long time, it was thought that these cells didn't have much of an effect on how the brain worked and how healthy it was. Ben's research changed this opinion and his discoveries have influenced many scientists' work since then.

Using His Platform

Ben was assigned female at birth, but always felt as though he was a boy trapped in a girl's body. He transitioned from female to male while working in a university. Having experienced it himself, Ben knows the barriers and challenges that many women and other <u>marginalised</u> groups working in STEM face. Because of this, he became an activist who tried to make the sciences a friendlier and more supportive place for women and marginalised people to work and study.

Stereotypes in STEM

It can be hard for some groups of people to feel welcomed, supported and respected in STEM. This might be because of stereotypes, having fewer opportunities or not having enough role models. Luckily, lots is being done to make working in STEM more inclusive.

- Has multiple awards named after him, supporting his work and the things he has achieved

- First transgender scientist in the National Academy of Sciences

- Awarded Stanford University President's Award for Excellence through Diversity in 2017

Be who you are, make sure you focus on all your talents and ... the rest will follow.

MEGAN SMITH

Born: 1964

> There are 2 to 3 million women <u>programmers</u> in the world. We need to see more of them.

> Talent is everywhere. Not all talent has <u>access</u>.

High Time for High Tech

Megan Smith became interested in STEM after her first <u>science fair</u>. After growing up and going to university, she had many jobs where she helped to develop high-tech products including some of the earliest smartphones and touchscreens. She then went on to work for several technology companies including Google.

Achievements

- First ever female US Chief Technology Officer

- Received an award from GLAAD for her advancing of LGBTQIA+ equality through technology

- Named as a pioneer by the World Economic Forum

FIGHT BACK!

Creating Spaces

Megan Smith is an openly gay woman and she does a lot of work to promote women in STEM roles. She is also a role model for the LGBTQIA+ community in STEM. In 2014, Barack Obama made her the Chief Technology Officer in the US. In every job she has done, she has used her position to make sure women and members of the LGBTQIA+ community have access and an interest in science and technology.

WOMEN IN STEM

ANN MEI CHANG

Born: 1967

A Tech Titan

Ann Mei Chang spent the first half of her career working in technology. She worked at companies including Apple and Google, where she helped to create lots of new technologies. She was then made the Senior Advisor for Women and Technology in the US where she worked to increase the representation of women in technology and make sure more women had access to technology (see page 21 to read more about representation).

A Change of Direction

After her work in technology, her career took a very different turn. Chang began working in **aid**. She uses her technological knowledge to help her make a difference across the world by supporting people who are starting new and original projects.

Using Your Differences to Your Advantage

Ann Mei Chang is a gay woman who talks about the importance of being yourself and finding out who your community is in anything that you do. She also talks about how working in technology has become easier for the LGBTQIA+ community and that lots of companies now support the community more.

> I wanted to spend the first half of my career in the tech world and the second half of my career doing something more meaningful.

Achievements

- Named as one of the 125 Women of Impact in 2013

- Named as one of the 23 most powerful LGBTQIA+ people in tech

WOMEN IN STEM

NERGIS MAVALVALA

Born: 1968

> Anybody should be able to succeed — whether you're a woman, a religious minority or whether you're gay. It just doesn't matter. Anybody should be able to do those things, and I am proof of that because I am all of those things.

A Universe Full of Questions

From a young age, Nergis remembers being interested in the universe and how it works. It is no surprise then that Nergis started looking into astrophysics. Her research mostly focuses on looking at the energy around large objects in space. She has even managed to show that many of Albert Einstein's ideas, which he formed over 100 years ago, were correct.

Out and Proud

Nergis is a role model for a lot of people in astrophysics. She is a woman who was born in Pakistan who also identifies as an 'out, queer person of colour'.
By being open about her sexuality and background, she shows that people can become anything they want to be.

An out, queer person of colour.

Achievements

- Won the LGBTQ Scientist of the Year Award from the National Organisation of Gay and Lesbian Scientists and Technical Professors in 2014

- Awarded the MacArthur Fellowship in 2010 for her scientific work

What Is Representation?

Representation is when lots of different types of people are shown in public. This might be in the <u>media</u>, in sports, or even in schools and communities. Different ages, <u>cultures</u>, sexes and abilities should be represented.

POLLY ARNOLD

Born: 1972

> I've always loved problem solving, and working with my hands, and I didn't want a desk job.

Nuclear Knowledge

Polly Arnold was interested in chemistry because it involved solving lots of problems. She has worked as a professor in many universities, both in the US and the UK. A lot of her work explores <u>nuclear</u> waste and what happens to it after a long period of time. She is also exploring ways we can deal with it better by using chemistry.

- Winner of the Rosalind Franklin Award in 2012 for her scientific work and promotion of women in science

- Awarded an OBE in 2017 for her contributions to chemistry and women in STEM

- Founder of SciSisters, a place for women in science to work together

Working for Women

Throughout her career, Polly has worked towards making the sciences a better place for women to work in. She is also openly bisexual and has become a role model for many LGBTQIA+ people looking to work in STEM. She often speaks openly about her experiences as both a woman and an LGBTQIA+ person working in STEM and hopes that this will encourage others to do the same.

AUDREY TANG

Born: 1981

> I recognise people by their values ... not their genders, or roles, ... I expect the same in return.

Childhood, Computers and Coding

Audrey Tang was very interested in computers and coding from a very young age. By the age of eight she had designed her first program, and at the age of 14 she dropped out of school to focus on programming and technology.

Taking Taiwan by Storm

Audrey is open about her gender identity and talks openly about her transition from male to female. Audrey also talks about how she feels that the world is becoming more post-gender. Taiwan appointed Audrey as their Digital Minister in order to revolutionise how the Taiwanese government approaches the digital world. As Digital Minister, Audrey has made technology more accessible for many people in Taiwan.

My gender is officially whatever.

- Became Taiwan's youngest government minister
- Became the first transgender minister in the world

What Is Non-Binary, Gender Fluid and Post-Gender?

Many people don't feel they are either masculine or feminine. These people might be non-binary, meaning they don't fit into either the masculine gender or the feminine gender. A person who is non-binary might see themselves as gender fluid. This means they might switch between genders, feeling more masculine one day, and then more feminine the next. Post-gender is the idea that the need to define people by genders no longer exists. People who see themselves as non-binary or post-gender might not want to use the pronouns he or she but prefer more inclusive terms such as they or them.

JACK ANDRAKA

Born: 1997

A Child Genius

Jack was always interested in the sciences, but after a close family friend died of a type of cancer that is hard to test for, Jack put his mind to creating a test that would help to identify the cancer earlier on. He succeeded in creating the test and in 2012, at the age of just 15, he won an award at the Intel International Science and Engineering Fair for his work.

Talking about Coming Out

Since Jack's rise to fame, he has been very open in talking about his sexuality. He hopes that by being openly gay and sharing his coming out story, he will become a role model for young LGBTQIA+ people. He also wants to show young people that their ideas are important and that they can make a difference in STEM from a young age.

I'm openly gay and one of my biggest hopes is that I can help inspire other LGBT youth to get involved in STEM. I didn't have many role models besides Alan Turing.

Achievements

- Won a prize at the 2012 Intel International Science and Engineering Fair at the age of just 15

- He has worked with many organisations to improve LGBTQIA+ inclusivity in STEM

- Awarded the Smithsonian American Ingenuity Award

BE AN ALLY!

You don't have to be a member of the LGBTQIA+ community to make sure that those who are feel safe and supported as a group. This is called being an ally. Here is how you can be an ally in STEM.

Ask All Different Types of People

When doing STEM activities, it can be easy to only think about how something would work best for you. Make sure you ask all different types of people about your ideas to make sure you aren't making anyone feel left out or excluded. It is good to share ideas and make sure you have thought about lots of ways of doing things and from lots of different viewpoints.

Be Inclusive

In everything you do, it is important to think about how your actions might make someone else feel. For example, if you are writing a questionnaire to see what people think of your STEM ideas, make sure there are boxes for 'they/them' and well as 'he' and 'she'. This way, everyone will feel included.

Make Sure Nobody Is Left Out

If you are in any STEM clubs, make sure that nobody is left out. Make sure that everyone gets a turn and a chance to take part. If you see someone being treated differently, make sure you tell an adult that you trust.

A HELPING HAND

There is lots of information online for people who might be questioning their sex, sexuality or gender identity. These websites are also useful to learn how to be a good ally. Here are some websites to take a look at.

www.glaad.org

GLAAD works towards making sure members of the LGBTQIA+ community are accepted and represented.

www.stonewall.org.uk

Stonewall works to protect the rights of LGBTQIA+ people, make the world more accepting of LGBTQIA+ rights and make sure companies and organisations value the knowledge and experience that the LGBTQIA+ community can bring to them.

www.500queerscientists.com

500 Queer Scientists is a campaign that aims to make queer people in STEM better represented.

www.itgetsbetter.org.uk

The It Gets Better Project aims to make sure that nobody who is a member of the LGBTQIA+ community feels as though they are alone. They also focus on sharing young people's experiences and empowering and encouraging them.

www.prideinstem.org

Pride in STEM is an organisation that helps to makes LGBTQIA+ people better known in STEM and to highlight the obstacles that the LGBTQIA+ community might face when learning STEM in school or working in STEM jobs.

GLOSSARY

access	already having ways and paths in place that allow someone to do or achieve something
activist	a person who tries to make a change in the world by doing things such as going to marches
AI	artificial intelligence; when a machine or computer tries to mimic how a human brain works by making decisions and reasoning on its own
aid	support, such as food or money, given by governments or charities in a time of disaster
assigned	to be given without having a choice
astrophysics	a type of science that studies stars and other objects in space
attracted	to want to form a close, romantic or sexual relationship with someone
biological sex	whether a person's sex characteristics are considered to be male, female or intersex
biology	the science that studies the growth and life processes of living things
cell	a basic unit that, along with other cells, makes up all living things
chromosomes	tiny things inside cells that give our bodies information about what to do and how to grow
cisgender	when a person's gender identity matches the biological sex they were assigned at birth
community	a group of people who are connected by something
computer chips	small electronic circuits inside a computer that make them work
cultures	the traditions, ideas and ways of life of different groups of people
equality	the state of being equal, having the same opportunities and rights as someone else
feminine	things that are stereotypically associated with being female
flourishing	doing well or excelling in a particular thing
gender fluid	when a person's gender can switch between masculine or feminine or be a mixture of both
genitals	parts of the body found between the legs
GLAAD	Gay & Lesbian Alliance Against Defamation, GLAAD is an organisation that makes sure the media covers LGBTQIA+ topics in the right way

heterosexual	only being attracted to people of the opposite sex to you
inclusive	making sure that everyone feels involved and included in an equal way
march	a large gathering of people who walk from one point to another in order to try to change or celebrate something
marginalised	to have been treated differently because you are on the edge of a group or different to the majority of people in a particular place or community
masculine	things that are stereotypically associated with being male
media	the different ways that information is shown to the public such as TV, adverts, newspapers and radio
minister	the name for the head of a department in government in some countries
NASA	the National Aeronautics and Space Administration, the US space agency
neurobiologist	a scientist who studies the system of nerves in the body
nuclear	a type of energy that is created by breaking apart atoms, which are the smallest building blocks of the universe
OBE	Officer of the Most Excellent Order of the British Empire, an award given to people who have made a great change in their community
obituary	a public announcement of someone's death
obstacles	things that might stop someone from doing something
opportunities	chances to do or take part in things
pansexual	when a person can be attracted to anyone regardless of their biological sex, sexuality, gender or gender identity
pardoned	to remove someone's conviction of a crime
physics	the scientific study of how matter and energy act and work including light, heat, sound and electricity
pioneer	the first person to do something new or in a new way
programmers	people who write instructions or codes for computers
represented	acted as a symbol for something else
revolutionise	to change how something has ever been done or thought of before
rights	the basic things that a person is legally entitled to have
science fair	an event and competition where different people present and explain scientific ideas
sex characteristics	behaviours or physical features that tell you of a person's biological sex
stereotypes	beliefs which are not founded in facts but are believed by a lot of people

INDEX